GW00503124

FRANCIS FRITH'S

RAMSGATE

PHOTOGRAPHIC MEMORIES

BARRIE WOOTTON was born in Edmonton, North London in 1942. His parents were born in Ramsgate, and he came to live in St Peter's, Thanet, in 1952. He attended St Peter's Boys' School and then Hereson School until the age of 13, when he transferred to the then new Charles Dickens School. On leaving school he served a 5-year apprenticeship as a Fitter, and in 1966 he joined Pfizer Ltd at Sandwich, Kent, where he worked for 34 years until taking early retirement. His interest in local history began 40 years ago, after being given some photographic postcards of Ramsgate by his father. This inspired him to go on collecting, and to research the history of Ramsgate, Broadstairs and St Peter's. After marrying June in 1965 Barrie moved to Sandwich. Barrie has also written 'Early Broadstairs and St Peter's' (1992), 'Ramsgate and St Lawrence' (1996), co-authored with Don Dimond, and 'Images of Thanet: the Photographs of Thomas Page Swaine' (2004).

FRANCIS FRITH'S
PHOTOGRAPHIC MEMORIES

RAMSGATE

PHOTOGRAPHIC MEMORIES

BARRIE WOOTTON

First published in the United Kingdom in 2005 by
Frith Book Company Ltd

Limited Hardback Edition Published in 2005
ISBN 1-85937-930-3

Paperback Edition Published in 2005
ISBN 1-85937-627-X

Text and Design copyright © Frith Book Company Ltd
Photographs copyright © The Francis Frith Collection

The Frith photographs and the Frith logo are reproduced under
licence from Heritage Photographic Resources Ltd, the owners of
the Frith archive and trademarks

All rights reserved. No photograph in this publication may be sold
to a third party other than in the original form of this publication,
or framed for sale to a third party. No parts of this publication may
be reproduced, stored in a retrieval system, or transmitted, in any
form, or by any means, electronic, mechanical, photocopying,
recording or otherwise, without the prior permission of the
publishers and copyright holder.

British Library Cataloguing in Publication Data

Francis Frith's Ramsgate - Photographic Memories
Barrie Wootton

Frith Book Company Ltd
Frith's Barn, Teffont,
Salisbury, Wiltshire SP3 5QP
Tel: +44 (0) 1722 716 376
Email: info@francisfrith.co.uk
www.francisfrith.co.uk

Printed and bound in Great Britain

Front Cover: **RAMSGATE**, *Harbour Parade and New Road c1920* 68467t
Frontispiece: **RAMSGATE**, *the Harbour Crosswall 1907* 58287

*The colour-tinting is for illustrative purposes only, and is not intended
to be historically accurate*

Acknowledgements
I should like to take the opportunity to thank the following people sincerely for their help and for the information they provided:
The staff of Ramsgate and Margate Libraries, especially Mrs Linda Kember; Mr Mick Twyman; Mr Terry Wheeler; Mr Don Dimond;
Mr John Williams; Mr Ian (Danny) Day; Mr Clive Baker; and Mr Matt Solomon of Carillion. Special thanks must go to Ms Dot Toft for
her shared interest, whether typing, proof reading or helping in constructing the text of this book. Lastly, my thanks also go to my
long-suffering wife for her forbearance during the many hours I have spent on this project. If I have inadvertently infringed any
copyright or made any factual errors in the information provided, my sincere apologies.

AS WITH ANY HISTORICAL DATABASE THE FRITH ARCHIVE IS CONSTANTLY
BEING CORRECTED AND IMPROVED AND THE PUBLISHERS WOULD WELCOME
INFORMATION ON OMISSIONS OR INACCURACIES

CONTENTS

FRANCIS FRITH
VICTORIAN PIONEER

FRANCIS FRITH, founder of the world-famous photographic archive, was a complex and multi-talented man. A devout Quaker and a highly successful Victorian businessman, he was philosophical by nature and pioneering in outlook.

By 1855 he had already established a wholesale grocery business in Liverpool, and sold it for the astonishing sum of £200,000, which is the equivalent today of over £15,000,000. Now a very rich man, he was able to indulge his passion for travel. As a child he had pored over travel books written by early explorers, and his fancy and imagination had been stirred by family holidays to the sublime mountain regions of Wales and Scotland. 'What lands of spirit-stirring and enriching scenes and places!' he had written. He was to return to these scenes of grandeur in later years to 'recapture the thousands of vivid and tender memories', but with a different purpose. Now in his thirties, and captivated by the new science of photography, Frith set out on a series of pioneering journeys up the Nile and to the Near East that occupied him from 1856 until 1860.

INTRIGUE AND EXPLORATION

These far-flung journeys were packed with intrigue and adventure. In his life story, written when he was sixty-three, Frith tells of being held captive by bandits, and of fighting 'an awful midnight battle to the very point of surrender with a deadly pack of hungry, wild dogs'. Wearing flowing Arab costume, Frith arrived at Akaba by camel sixty years before Lawrence of Arabia, where he encountered 'desert princes and rival sheikhs, blazing with jewel-hilted swords'.

He was the first photographer to venture beyond the sixth cataract of the Nile. Africa was still the mysterious 'Dark Continent', and Stanley and Livingstone's historic meeting was a decade into the future. The conditions for picture taking confound belief. He laboured for hours in his wicker dark-room in the sweltering heat of the desert, while the volatile chemicals fizzed dangerously in their trays. Back in London he exhibited his photographs and was 'rapturously cheered' by members of the Royal Society. His reputation as a photographer was made overnight.

VENTURE OF A LIFE-TIME

Characteristically, Frith quickly spotted the opportunity to create a new business as a specialist publisher of photographs. He lived in an era of immense and sometimes violent change.

For the poor in the early part of Victoria's reign work was exhausting and the hours long, and people had precious little free time to enjoy themselves. Most had no transport other than a cart or gig at their disposal, and rarely travelled far beyond the boundaries of their own town or village. However, by the 1870s the railways had threaded their way across the country, and Bank Holidays and half-day Saturdays had been made obligatory by Act of Parliament. All of a sudden the working man and his family were able to enjoy days out and see a little more of the world.

With typical business acumen, Francis Frith foresaw that these new tourists would enjoy having souvenirs to commemorate their days out. In 1860 he married Mary Ann Rosling and set out on a new career: his aim was to photograph every city, town and village in Britain. For the next thirty years he travelled the country by train and by pony and trap, producing fine photographs of seaside resorts and beauty spots that were keenly bought by millions of Victorians. These prints were painstakingly pasted into family albums and pored over during the dark nights of winter, rekindling precious memories of summer excursions.

THE RISE OF FRITH & CO

Frith's studio was soon supplying retail shops all over the country. To meet the demand he gathered about him a small team of photographers, and published the work of independent artist-photographers of the calibre of Roger Fenton and Francis Bedford. In order to gain some understanding of the scale of Frith's business one only has to look at the catalogue issued by Frith & Co in 1886: it runs to some 670 pages, listing not only many thousands of views of the British Isles but also many photographs of most European countries, and China, Japan, the USA and Canada - note the sample page shown on page 9 from the hand-written Frith & Co ledgers recording the pictures. By 1890 Frith had created the greatest specialist photographic publishing company in the world, with over 2,000 sales outlets - more than the combined number that Boots and WH Smith have today! The picture on the next page shows the Frith & Co display board at Ingleton in the Yorkshire Dales (left of window). Beautifully constructed with a mahogany frame and gilt inserts, it could display up to a dozen local scenes.

POSTCARD BONANZA

The ever-popular holiday postcard we know today took many years to develop. In 1870 the Post Office issued the first plain cards, with a pre-printed stamp on one face. In 1894 they allowed other publishers' cards to be sent through the mail with an attached adhesive halfpenny stamp. Demand grew rapidly, and in 1895 a new size of postcard was permitted called the court card, but there was little room for illustration. In 1899, a year after Frith's death, a new card measuring 5.5 x 3.5 inches became the standard format, but it was not until 1902 that the divided back came into being, so that the address and message could be on one face and a full-size illustration on the other. Frith & Co were in the vanguard of postcard development: Frith's sons Eustace and Cyril continued their father's monumental task, expanding the number of views offered to the public and recording more and more places in Britain, as the

St Catherine's College
Senate House & Library
Gerard Hostel Bridge
Geological Museum
Addenbrooke's Hospital
St Mary's Church
Fitzwilliam Museum, Pitt Press &c
Buxton, The Crescent
The Colonnade
Public Gardens
Haddon Hall, View from the Terrace
Miller's Dale

coasts and countryside were opened up to mass travel.

Francis Frith had died in 1898 at his villa in Cannes, his great project still growing. The archive he created continued in business for another seventy years. By 1970 it contained over a third of a million pictures showing 7,000 British towns and villages.

FRANCIS FRITH'S LEGACY

Frith's legacy to us today is of immense significance and value, for the magnificent archive of evocative photographs he created provides a unique record of change in the cities, towns and villages throughout Britain over a century and more. Frith and his fellow studio photographers revisited locations many times down the years to update their views, compiling for us an enthralling and colourful pageant of British life and character.

We are fortunate that Frith was dedicated to recording the minutiae of everyday life. For it is this sheer wealth of visual data, the painstaking chronicle of changes in dress, transport, street layouts, buildings, housing, engineering and landscape that captivates us so much today. His remarkable images offer us a powerful link with the past and with the lives of our ancestors.

THE VALUE OF THE ARCHIVE TODAY

Computers have now made it possible for Frith's many thousands of images to be accessed almost instantly. Frith's images are increasingly used as visual resources, by social historians, by researchers into genealogy and ancestry, by architects and town planners, and by teachers involved in local history projects.

In addition, the archive offers every one of us an opportunity to examine the places where we and our families have lived and worked down the years. Highly successful in Frith's own era, the archive is now, a century and more on, entering a new phase of popularity. Historians consider the Francis Frith Collection to be of prime national importance. It is the only archive of its kind remaining in private ownership. Francis Frith's archive is now housed in an historic timber barn in the beautiful village of Teffont in Wiltshire. Its founder would not recognize the archive office as it is today. In place of the many thousands of dusty boxes containing glass plate negatives and an all-pervading odour of photographic chemicals, there are now ranks of computer screens. He would be amazed to watch his images travelling round the world at unimaginable speeds through internet lines.

The archive's future is both bright and exciting. Francis Frith, with his unshakeable belief in making photographs available to the greatest number of people, would undoubtedly approve of what is being done today with his lifetime's work. His photographs depicting our shared past are now bringing pleasure and enlightenment to millions around the world a century and more after his death.

RAMSGATE
AN INTRODUCTION

IN THE EARLY YEARS of the parish of St Laurence, Ramsgate did not exist. In its place was an opening between high cliffs which allowed surface water to drain from the upper areas of Westcliff, East Cliff, Northwood and Southwood. These waters formed a small stream, which followed a gentle slope to the seashore—the High Street approximately follows its course today. On reaching the cross roads where King Street and Queen Street meet, the ground levels out; the water spread, and created a marshy pond area where the old Town Hall and market place once stood. The pond or marsh then drained to the sea. Indeed, there has always been flooding at this cross roads during my lifetime.

The derivation of Ramsgate's name is interesting. The word 'gate' is an old Celtic word for 'an opening in the cliff'. Secondly, the word

RAMSGATE, *The Beach c1880* 12731

'rhuim' is said to mean 'forest', and there were forests here, as we can see from the names Northwood, Southwood and Westwood. A similar word, 'rhuime', could also mean 'moor or marsh'. Thus 'Ramsgate' could be interpreted as 'marsh by the gap in the cliffs' or 'forest by the gap in the cliffs'. The first use of the name Ramsgate that we know of appears in the records of the Court of the Hundred of Ringslow in 1274, of which the parish of St Laurence was a member. Here a family consisting of Martin Stephen Bartholomew, Baldwin Johanna and Clement De Ramsgate all paid a tax called 'Romescot' to the Abbot of St Augustine's monastery.

Ramsgate is situated on the south-east coast of the Isle of Thanet, and its history is entwined with that of Thanet. The Wansum Channel separated Thanet from the mainland of Kent, and the island was a stepping-stone to Britain for invaders and travellers from the Continent.

'Richardson's Fragments of History' quotes the Dean of Westminster as saying in his 'Memorials of Canterbury' that of the five great landings in English history, the first three and most important are said to have taken place in Kent. The first was the landing of Julius Caesar at Deal in 55 BC, the second was that of Hengist and Horsa in AD 449, and the third was the arrival of St Augustine in AD 597. My opinion is that the significant Roman invasion is the one of AD 43, when the Roman general Aulus Plautius landed on the small island of Rutupiae in the Wansum Channel unopposed and conquered Thanet, south-east Kent and later southern England, laying the basis for the Roman occupation of Britain. Hengist and Horsa gave us the foundation of our English heritage; we are told that they landed at Ebbsfleet, which is within Ramsgate's

present boundaries. Finally, St Augustine landed at the same place—he gave us Christianity.

Augustine (later to be made a saint) established two great seats of religious thought. One was at Canterbury, where he lived, and the other was at Minster, then the capital of Thanet. The important Convent of St Mary was built in AD 670, and exercised its ecclesiastical rule over Thanet. History is not clear as to how or exactly when other chapels were established in Thanet, but by the 11th century, and before the Norman Conquest, there existed five major chapels, those of St Laurence, St Peter and St John and two others. These chapels were visited by monks from either Minster or Canterbury who ministered to these sparsely populated areas where dwellings were clustered around each chapel. It is strange that St Peter's became the first parochial village in 1200; it was not until 1275 that St Laurence achieved this status. For the purpose of this book we shall concentrate on the parish of St Laurence.

In the 11th century, the parish of St Laurence covered a large area, and consisted of two large manors, Upper Court and Nethercourt, plus Osengall Grange. A few fishermen's huts stood by a gap in the cliffs leading to the sea. Those living by the sea augmented their summer farm work with fishing during the winter months. By the 14th century a small breakwater had been built; it was later to be enlarged to a small harbour, which attracted the attention of Sandwich, a major Cinque Port. Ramsgate became a Limb of Liberty of the Confederation of Cinque Ports, and enjoyed the attendant privileges which went with this. Sandwich's interest centred on the small harbour, which was capable of giving shelter to channel shipping. In fewer than 200 years,

Sandwich would almost cease to be a sea port owing to silting. Ramsgate, however, had clear access to the sea and fostered trade from Russia and the Baltic countries; it would go on to achieve greater power and expansion.

In 1749, Ramsgate was chosen as the site for a new harbour, with the proviso that it set aside a sum of money to keep Sandwich clear of silt. The harbour repaid its construction costs by becoming a major troop embarkation port during the Napoleonic wars. It was reported that the trade of foying or hovelling (doing any kind of work on the coast) for the East India Company by Ramsgate, Margate and Broadstairs men brought all three towns the sum of between £50,000 and £60,000 in one year. The shipment of troops to France in turn saw large outlying areas of the existing town used as barracks;

Spencer Square and Wellington Crescent, built up later, stand on the spot.

The close proximity of the Goodwin Sands to Ramsgate has meant that men of the town have always risked their lives to rescue mariners from these treacherous waters. Ramsgate has strong links with the lifeboat service, for it was here in 1785 that Lionel Lukin tested his first unimmergible boat. It is ironic that this boat was later confiscated and burnt because of its use in smuggling. Ramsgate Lifeboat Station is one of the oldest in the country—it was established in 1802. Many of Ramsgate's lifeboat coxswains hold RNLI medals for bravery.

In 1821, King George IV left Ramsgate harbour for Hanover. He received a warm send-off and later again a warm welcome on his return from the inhabitants of Ramsgate; he was so

RAMSGATE, *From Albion Place c1912* 68462

pleased with his reception, that he decreed that Ramsgate harbour should be designated Royal. In 1823, an obelisk was built and unveiled to celebrate this visit. Even greater good fortune was to befall the town: the Duke of Clarence (later King William IV), one of George IV's friends, enjoyed the company of a Miss Long, who lived in Ramsgate Town. As a young girl Princess Victoria enjoyed many happy hours of pleasure on the sands before becoming sovereign queen.

The parish of St Laurence still governed Ramsgate until 1827, when Ramsgate's St George's Parish Church was built, and a local act for separating the town from the parish of St Laurence was granted. However, Ramsgate was still not its own master, because its civic control was administered from Sandwich. Ramsgate sands and the surrounding area made it fashionable as a holiday destination, and access to Ramsgate was made even easier and cheaper by the arrival of the South Eastern Railway in April 1846. In 1863, the London, Chatham & Dover Railway ran a new line along the Kent coast; not only did this make the journey shorter, but the LCDR also deposited its travellers at a new station within 50 yards of the sands.

On 21 March 1884, Ramsgate officially became a borough, and finally severed its ties with Sandwich. Its first mayor was John Kennett Esq of Nethercourt; his mayoral chain was presented to the town by Sir Moses Montefiore, the great Jewish benefactor, who at the time of the presentation was 100 years old—he lived on the East Cliff in East Cliff Lodge. Furthermore, Thomson & Wotton, the Ramsgate brewers, presented the town with its mace. Ramsgate was granted a coat of arms by the College of Heralds.

The seaside holiday trade of the 1880s was recorded as being the busiest in the town's history, and certainly the building of the Granville Hotel by Augustus Welby Pugin attracted many London-based travellers so strongly that a special train named 'The Granville Express' was organised. This train made the journey from London to Ramsgate in under two hours. In April 1901, local transport between Ramsgate, Margate and Broadstairs was vastly improved by the implementation of the local tramways (whose depot was at St Peter's). As a result, Ramsgate achieved a holiday resort status closely likened to Blackpool and Brighton during Queen Victoria's reign. Many of the royal family performed opening ceremonies of various public buildings in and around Ramsgate; a particular instance is the opening of the Royal Victoria Pavilion by Princess Louise on 29 June 1904.

With the advent of the harbour, the fishing trade of Ramsgate had begun to expand. By the turn of the 20th century, Ramsgate had a large fishing fleet, but with the coming World War I, the fleet was to be dispersed to other ports, and suffered great losses to German submarines or mines. The harbour became a naval station for the famous Dover Patrol, which was created to keep the English Channel clear of enemy vessels and mines. The town was one of the first to be exposed to the then new horror of air raids by Zeppelin airships and aircraft, which it bore with true 'British bulldog' stoicism. Ramsgate became an important frontline port during the hostilities. The cessation of World War I saw Ramsgate return to its former seaside glories and further development. Unfortunately, the fishing fleet was never to return to its previous peak, but the holiday trade soon came back, exceeding its pre-war standing. In 1935, under a County

Review Order, Ramsgate Borough boundary was extended to include the whole of St Laurence. The wheel had turned full circle. Nine centuries earlier, St Laurence had encompassed what was to become the town; now it was within the Parish of Ramsgate.

The Sands railway station, which closed during 1926, was turned into a large amusement park called 'Pleasureland' and later 'Merry England'. Furthermore, the outlying areas of Ramsgate were developed into housing, and the ancient tramway system was replaced by the far-reaching and more up-to-date East Kent bus service in 1937. After 26 years of peace, war clouds loomed in 1938 with the Munich Agreement. With the outbreak of World War II in September 1939, Ramsgate harbour was again turned into a naval station, HMS Fervent, and was soon to be used in the forefront of the famous Dunkirk retreat, Operation Dynamo. Thousands of troops were to reach the safe haven of this harbour to fight another day. As it had been during World War I, Ramsgate was again shelled and bombed by the enemy. A well-remembered wartime personality is Ramsgate's 'top hat' mayor, Alderman A B C Kemp, who was mayor elect for a record five years from 1938 to 1942. The harbour became an air-sea rescue station, saving many pilots from Davy Jones's locker. Sons and daughters of local families paid the ultimate sacrifice for today's freedom.

Ramsgate returned to some normality after 6 years of strife. On 28 July 1949, the Viking ship 'Hugin' landed at Broadstairs in celebration of the 1500th anniversary of the landing of Hengist and Horsa at Ebbsfleet, and the following day its first visit was to Ramsgate, where it received a tumultuous reception. Later, after touring various ports in Britain, this replica was bought by the Daily Mail newspaper and presented to Broadstairs and Ramsgate, who chose to place it at Pegwell Bay, not far from where its original ancestors had

RAMSGATE, *Dumpton Gap 1894* 34194

landed at Ebbsfleet. The period of the last 50 years has brought about wear and tear and social change to Ramsgate, just as it has to the 'Hugin'. One momentous change was in 1974, when local authority was vested in Thanet District Council; this made the Ramsgate and Margate Borough Councils redundant, along with Broadstairs and St Peter's Urban District Council.

Ramsgate's expanded harbour is now a marina for private yachts and motor cruisers, which shares facilities with a commercial ferry line, a far call from its fishing fleet origins. The expansion of Ramsgate town is now directed out to the acres of farmland which used to lie between its neighbours Margate and Broadstairs. A shopping centre, Westwood Cross, is now being erected in these vacated spaces. Even the Merry England/Pleasurama amusement arcades, which mysteriously burnt down, are to be developed into a hotel and apartment complex. The holiday resort of Ramsgate is marketed as part of Thanet. Whether this is good or bad, who can tell? But while ink is in the pen, or fingers on the computer keyboard, people will continue to write about the many accomplished deeds and stories of Ramsgate and its townsfolk.

RAMSGATE, *Inner Basin and Harbour Parade 1857* ZZZ03382

17

MINSTER AND MONKTON

MINSTER-IN-THANET, *The Abbey 1894* 34200

The abbey stands on the site of a Saxon nunnery set up by Domneva, and run by St Augustine's monks from Canterbury; it was destroyed in the ninth century by the invading Danes. Rebuilding started in the 11th century. The year 1538 saw the Dissolution of the Monasteries by King Henry VIII, and the land reverted to the Crown. Later, ownership of the grounds went to the Conyngham family and various tenant farmers until 1937, when a community of German Benedictine nuns bought the monastery and 10 acres of land.

MINSTER-IN-THANET
The Abbey c1955
M86031

The abbey, the oldest building in Minster, is to be found at the lower end of the village. Before 1937, it had been called Minster Court; it was one of the oldest occupied buildings in the country, at one time owned by the Swynford family. The abbey is now a working farm, still run by the Benedictine nuns.

MINSTER-IN-THANET, *St Mary's Church, the Interior 1894* 34205

Minster was once the ancient capital of Thanet. It was a small quiet village, and used to govern the hamlets of St Laurence, St Peter and St John. Because the church was one of the most important buildings in the community, the nave may have served as a storehouse, a courthouse and even as a place of refuge in earlier times.

19

◄ **MINSTER-IN-THANET**
*St Mary's Church,
the Interior c2004*
ZZZ03361

This shows the choir stalls
and the altar. The church
has changed very little in
the last 60 years, apart from
the use of electricity as
against gas lamps.

◀ **MINSTER-IN-THANET**
St Mary's Church c1955
M86030

St Mary's is built on the former site of Domneva's nunnery, which was established about AD 670. Parts of the building date back to 1160. The building to the right is the old village school, now a meeting room.

▲ **MINSTER-IN-THANET,** *St Mary's Church 2004* ZZZ03362

Today's view of St Mary's is partially obscured by large trees. The village school is still here, but it has unfortunately lost its school bell. When this photograph was taken, the church gates had been removed for repair, but they are still part of the main fabric of the church.

◀ **MONKTON**
Thatched Cottage c1960 M257012

When this photograph was taken, the occupant was Reginald Fasham. In 1928, the cottage was named The Croft, and was home to Wilfred Fitzmaurice Morris.

► **MONKTON**
The Post Office
c1955 M257010

This house was still a post office at this time. In 1928, the post office and grocery was run by Thomas Stephen Smith. It continued as a post office and grocery, and in 1948 Percy George Jarvis ran the establishment for at least 20 years. Next door, to the left, is the Old Forge, later Drake & Fletcher Ltd, agricultural engineers.

◄ **MONKTON**
The Old Post Office
2004 ZZZ03364

The house is now a private residence, and no-one would guess that this was once a very important part of Monkton village. The Old Forge has been demolished and replaced by another house, which stands on what was one of the focal points in the village .

▲ **MONKTON,** *Thatched Cottage 2004* ZZZ03363

There has been little change to this beautiful home (see photograph M257012, page 21). The loss of the mast in the garden at the rear, now planted with trees, only adds to the rustic appearance of this cottage. Even the car parked by the window goes to show that nothing changes in 44 years.

◄ **MINSTER-IN-THANET**
The Square c1960
M86035

This view was taken at the top of the High Street. In the centre is the New Inn public house and tea gardens, formerly owned by Cobbs' Brewery. In 1910 the owner, Mr J Easton, reared a duck which laid an egg weighing 8 ounces and measuring 10½ inches by 9 inches! To the left is the Monkton Road, and on the right is Tothill Street.

MINSTER-IN-THANET
The Square 2004 ZZZ03365

The buildings depicted have changed very little over the years, but the New Inn no longer operates a tea garden, nor is it part of Cobbs' Brewery, which has ceased to operate. The roads are now more congested with motor cars, although the pub is still a popular meeting place for residents and visitors.

MINSTER-IN-THANET, *High Street c1955* M86013

This view shows R E Attwell's to the right, which was the village newsagent's and tobacconist's; the proprietor was Chairman of Minster Parish Council. Two doors away at 55 High Street, previously known as Victoria Villas, was T H Webb the grocer's, which used these premises from 1928 until 1970.

MINSTER-IN-THANET
High Street 2004 ZZZ03366

Today, the High Street is a busy thoroughfare, and R E Attwell's is now run by his son, Mr Clive Attwell. Mr Attwell Senior had two terms of office as Chairman of the Parish Council, 1958-60 and 1962-64.

MINSTER-IN-THANET, *Buttsfield Estate c1955* M86002

Every village throughout England in the 1950s found an increase in population, and council estates were built on the green countryside. Minster was no exception, as we can see in this photograph. This estate was built after 1951; it was formerly the site of a mixed orchard, whose produce was sold through a greengrocer in Minster High Street.

MINSTER-IN-THANET
Buttsfield Estate 2004
ZZZ03367

Not only is there an increase in the ownership of cars visible in this view, but also most noticeable is the growth of small trees and hedges which obscure the number of buildings.

MINSTER-IN-THANET, *The Corner House Café c1960* M86050

The aptly-named Corner House Café was a confectioner's in 1948. Later, in 1960, a café was added to the business. It became the meeting place for most Minster teenagers, serving only coffee and sweets. It stood on the corner of Station Road and St Mildred's Road, known by older villagers as Vicarage Lane.

MINSTER-IN-THANET
Morton's Fork Hotel 2004 ZZZ03368

Today, there is no café or shop; instead Morton's Fork restaurant
and hotel occupies the site. Earlier, in 1900, Youngs the pork
butcher's stood where this establishment is located.

PEGWELL BAY

PEGWELL, *The 'Hugin' c1950* ZZZ03369

Landlocked, the 'Hugin' finds her final resting place
overlooking Pegwell Bay, less than one mile from the
original site where Hengist and Horsa first set foot on the
Isle of Thanet. This boat stands 50 yards from the busy A256
road from Ramsgate to Sandwich.

PEGWELL
The 'Hugin' 2004
ZZZ03370

On Wednesday 8 December 2004, the weather-ravaged 'Hugin' begins its long journey to Gloucester Docks with the aid of modern technology. The company assigned with the repair and ultimate return of one of Ramsgate's tourist gems is Tommie Nielsen & Co Ltd. Is it coincidence that this boat is entrusted to a son of the birthplace of its forebears, or are Hengist and Horsa keeping a watch on their descendants?

PEGWELL, *The Cliffs c1930* 68476

We are looking towards Pegwell village, with the footpath clearly visible, highlighted by the telegraph poles erected on its left-hand side. In the background are the coastguard cottages. In ancient times Pegwell was called Courtstairs, and was once a small manor attached to the Sheriffs Court in Minster parish. Beyond Cliffs End there are no more cliffs—hence its name.

PEGWELL
Pegwell Bay 1907 58300

Pegwell village overlooks a large bay, which has in the past been named Hope Bay, Greystone Bay, and Courtstairs Bay, and today is simply known as Pegwell Bay. The wooden steps give access to the ground below and also serve as a lookout tower for the coastguard station, and pictured below is a coastguard cutter on davits ready for any emergencies. The gardens beyond belonged to the Conyngham Hotel.

▶ **PEGWELL**
The Sea Front 1907
58299

Here we have a closer view of the wall and walk built from the cliff opposite, encompassing the ground later laid out as gardens, and earlier as a swimming pool, by the Pegwell Bay Reclamation Co. The gardens were known as Ravens Cliff Gardens. Also built on this reclaimed land was the Conyngham Hotel; access to it was gained via steps from the bay.

◀ **PEGWELL**
The Convalescent Home 1907 58301

This is a closer view of the Conyngham Restaurant with its extensive well laid-out grounds, which include swings and other children's facilities. Behind is the tall tower of the Working Men's Club and Institute Union Convalescent Home, once the Clifton Hotel; the tower and the new wing were added in 1897. On the extreme right are the stumps of an earlier pier, built by Daniel Curling in 1784.

▲ **PEGWELL,** *Pegwell Bay 1907* 58304

This Edwardian view shows the footpath to Pegwell village; on the extreme left are the coastguard cottages, built to prevent the extensive smuggling activities that were then carried out at this isolated location. Throughout the 1820s many people here watched regattas under the patronage of Earl Darnley and Mr Warre, when purses of gold sovereigns were given as prizes to the participants in yacht races.

◄ **PEGWELL**
High Street 1907 58297

On the right is the old Belle Vue Tavern dating back to the 1760s, which was an earlier haunt for smugglers. In 1831, the landlord Mr John Cramp received a visit from the Duchess of Kent and her daughter Princess Victoria; they dined on potted shrimp paste. Later, Mr Cramp received the Royal Appointment of Purveyor of Essence of Shrimps in Ordinary to Her Majesty the Queen. On the left are the Floral Tea Gardens followed by the Pear Tree Inn, later Samuel Banger's potted shrimp paste factory. His small paste pots had highly decorated lids depicting scenes of Pegwell; today they are valuable antiques.

WEST CLIFF

RAMSGATE, *Postcard Design c1960* R7072

This postcard typifies Ramsgate at the height of its holiday seaside popularity, when it challenged the renown of Blackpool with its lights and entertainment. Ramsgate at this time was very much the British holidaymakers 'cup of tea' before the advent of foreign travel.

RAMSGATE
St Laurence High Street 1910 ZZZ03371

Today nearly all of these buildings have gone; various clearance schemes have seen this road widened threefold. The only building existing today is the imposing structure facing us at the end of the road. This is the Wheatsheaf public house. This tranquil scene of horse-drawn vehicles, small shops, and stables (to the left) is something that we yearn for in today's non-stop noise.

RAMSGATE, *St Laurence's Church 1908* ZZZ03372

The chancel, nave and tower date back to 1062, making this the oldest of the three Thanet churches paying tithes to the mother church at Minster. St Laurence became a parish in 1275, and was responsible for the running of the ville of Ramsgate until 1827, when Ramsgate became a parish by an Act of Separation. On the extreme right in the background is the White Horse public house, which was demolished to widen the High Street.

RAMSGATE, *Ellington Park, the Fountain 1907* 58282

Ellington grounds were bought by Ramsgate Corporation in 1892 for £12,000, and were laid out by Cheal & Son. It opened on 7 September 1893 as Ellington Park, and this beautiful ornamental fountain was installed in 1895 as a gift from a former Burgess of Ramsgate, Mrs Barber, in memory of her son. It has been demolished, sad to say, and today is only a memory for older residents.

RAMSGATE, *Ellington Park, the Bandstand 1901* 48047X

The centre of attraction around which Ramsgate visitors and residents once clustered to listen to regimental and dance bands perform during 1920s and 1930s, the bandstand has survived two World Wars and countless vandals, and is still a focal point for musical experience.

RAMSGATE
*The Ramsgate Pageant
1934* ZZZ03373

This event was held in Ellington Park from 16 to 21 July 1934 to celebrate Ramsgate being made a Borough 50 years previously. The cast numbered 4,000, and local musicians produced the music. As we can see, this was a popular event, judging by the crowds watching the Elizabethan scene.

RAMSGATE, *Ramsgate Town Station 1925* ZZZ03374

This view shows the new Town Station at St Laurence under construction in 1925. Note the 1920s Port-a-loo in the foreground! In 1926, the country was paralysed by the National Strike. Ramsgate also closed the Sands Station and the old Town Station at Chatham Street. Furthermore, one new station opened at St Laurence and another at Dumpton Park.

RAMSGATE
The Old Town Station
1926 ZZZ03375

Ramsgate's first station was opened by the South Eastern & Chatham Railway in 1846. Along with the Sands, they closed on the same day, to be replaced by the two new stations the following morning without any interruption to services. The St Laurence Station took the place of this old Victorian building, running trains to Margate via Broadstairs. Previously, trains from this station ran direct to Margate.

RAMSGATE, *The Hotel de Ville c1900* ZZZ03376

This French name means 'Town Hall', so perhaps it is no surprise that this building was used for inquests in the early 1900s. Two former landlords committed suicide on the premises. The building is situated on the corner of Wilsons Road; it began its life as a licensed hotel. One of its famous patrons was the late John Le Mesurier, and one of its former owners was Lord George Sanger.

RAMSGATE, *Westcliff Windmill 1901* 48045

Standing on the corner of Canonbury Road and Grange Road, this windmill has a fascinating history. Originally built on the East Cliff, it was dismantled and erected on this site in 1810 by John Marshall. It was last used in 1913, and partially demolished in 1927; the base was used as a garage before its demolition in 1930.

RAMSGATE
Christ Church, Vale Square c1870 ZZZ03377

Built on ground once known as The Vale by William Saxby, Christ Church was opened
for services in 1847. William Saxby also built the Congregational church in Meeting Street.
Christ Church is built of Caen stone and Kentish ragstone, topped off with a steeple
covered in oak shingles.

RAMSGATE
Spencer Square 1890
27456

Work on building this elegant square started in 1802 after James Townley bought the ground. The buildings on the left were officers' quarters during the Napoleonic Wars. The square was a large parade ground, and nearby Addington Street was a military camp. Frith's photographer was standing outside No 6 Royal Road, where Vincent Van Gogh had stayed.

RAMSGATE, *Addington Street 1900* ZZZ03378

Seen here decked overall to celebrate the Relief of Mafeking in May 1900, the street is a hive of activity, with Union Jacks everywhere; giant Chinese lanterns add to the gaiety of the joyous scene. The street takes its name from Henry Sidmouth, later Lord Addington, a former British Prime Minister.

THE HARBOUR

RAMSGATE, *The Old Admiral Harvey 1890* ZZZ03379

This public house was demolished in 1902 and rebuilt further back on Harbour Parade. It once stood back to back with Dysons Royal Clarence Baths, patronised by King William IV. The pub was named after Admiral Henry Harvey (1737-1810), brother of a former vicar of St Laurence's Church.

RAMSGATE
The Harbour 1876 R7301

The two sluice gates were installed at Smeaton's request so as to scour away the outer Harbour's constant bogey—silt. Moored between these gates is a sailing bark, and in the distance can be seen the East and West Piers. Later, the eastern pier on the left would have a wooden landing stage added to allow London paddle steamers to moor up and disgorge their passengers.

RAMSGATE, *The Harbour 1857* ZZZ03380

Here we have a tranquil view at low water of the inner basin. On the extreme right is the Clock House. To its left in Smeaton's dry dock is a sailing vessel being repaired. The fishing smacks in the foreground have RE numbers, denoting that they are registered in Ramsgate; later the E was dropped and only the letter R used.

RAMSGATE
The Harbour 1907 58290

This photograph was taken from a slightly different angle from photograph R7301 (page 45) and on a much busier day. The bucket dredger 'Hope', which arrived in 1888, was later replaced by a grab-type dredger, the 'Ramsgate', at the end of the Second World War. To the right are two mud hoppers, whilst one fishing smack sails through the open sluice gate.

▶ **RAMSGATE**
The Harbour from West Cliff 1887 19674a

Here we see the inner harbour with its busy waterfront. On the extreme right are the police offices (a very small building) and next come the warehouses in the pier yard, demolished in 1890 to widen access to the Sands station. Opposite the police station is the Alexandra public house, and to its left the Castle and Royal Oak hotels, both registered in the 1770 rate book. The paddle steamer is the 'Queen of Thanet', owned by Ramsgate Steam Company. The Albion Hotel behind was partially demolished in 1892 to allow Madeira Walk to be constructed.

◀ **RAMSGATE**
The Inner Basin 1895 35871

Two interesting developments appear here. On the right, the dry dock has been half filled in by Thanet Ice Company, and an ice house has been built to supply ice to the fishing smacks. On the left, Harbour Parade and Military Road have been widened and raised. Madeira Walk was officially opened on 6 April 1895.

▲ RAMSGATE, *The Arrival of the 'Hugin' 1949* ZZZ03381

The replica Viking ship 'Hugin' lies safely in Ramsgate's inner basin on Friday 29 July 1949, after arriving at Broadstairs the previous day to be greeted by a crowd of 30,000 onlookers. The reception for the 'Hugin' was no less enthusiastic at Ramsgate than at Broadstairs, for everyone wanted to see this 'wooden wonder'. Moored against the quay in the background is one of the many timber boats that visited Ramsgate after the war.

◄ RAMSGATE
The Inner Harbour 1955
R7013

This modern view of the inner basin and Military Road is interesting for two reasons: the construction of the new road brought a number of maritime business premises to Military Road, which has been widened considerably; and this post-war photograph also shows a number of ex-Naval converted motor boats moored in the harbour.

RAMSGATE
*The Harbour Cross
Wall 1907* 58287

This view of the middle wall
of the harbour shows a
typical Edwardian mother
and her two children posing
for the photographer.
Behind her the busy life of
the harbour continues.
Many horse-drawn carts are
transferring freight from the
sailing vessel moored on the
quay. To the right is the
'Lord Warden' sailing barge,
and behind her is the old
fish market, which was
destroyed in World War I.

RAMSGATE
Inner Basin and Harbour Parade 1857 ZZZ03382

This view was taken from the harbour middle wall, and shows what was once known as the
Waterside, and is now Harbour Parade. From left to right, we see York Street, the Admiral Harvey,
Brockman's Dining Rooms, Stockbridge's bakery, Dyson's Royal Clarence Baths, the Royal Hotel,
then Harbour Street, and lastly the Albion Hotel. Today, hardly any of these buildings exist.
The fishing smack DH60 was registered at Brixham, Devon.

RAMSGATE
Replica of the 'Bounty' 1950 ZZZ03383

Originally the 'Alston', this vessel was moored next to the dry dock in 1947 and used as
a floating restaurant. Unfortunately, this venture was unsuccessful, and in 1951 the
'Bounty' was towed away and later broken up at Grays, Essex.

▼ **RAMSGATE,** *Bow of the 'Bounty' 1950* ZZZ03384

Advertised as a replica of the 'Bounty', this ship was one of the earlier attempts to use the harbour commercially in the post-war period. The 'Bounty' catered for parties of up to 120, and also for amusements and exhibitions. Today, I am sure it would have been a great success, but it was not so in the early 1950s, sad to say.

► **RAMSGATE**
The 'New Moss Rose'
1910 ZZZ03386

Depicted against the East Pier head, this vessel was popular with most visitors to Ramsgate who wished to test their sea legs and in some cases feed the fishes. The vessel is seen here under way without the help of either the 'Vulcan' or the 'Aid' tug.

◀ **RAMSGATE**
East Pier 1900 ZZZ03385

This late Victorian view shows what any passenger arriving by paddle steamer would see once they disembarked. Already there is a cluster of people waiting at the head of the steps which descended to the awaiting sail-powered pleasure boats. In the background is the panorama of Ramsgate's seafront.

▶ **RAMSGATE**
Harbour Parade and New Road 1901 48028

Gone are the sailing vessels, and in their place are the fishing smacks of the town. Furthermore, we can see a row of horse-drawn brakes, which shows that the tourist trade was expanding. These brakes were the only means of transporting the tourist to places such as Pegwell Bay or Minster; although these were popular venues, there were no tram services to these villages.

RAMSGATE
*Harbour Parade and
New Road c1920* 68467

Here we see the same view as
48028 (page 55) about twenty
years on. The First World War
saw the demise of the
Ramsgate fishing fleet;
indeed, in this photograph
we can see that the smacks
have all but disappeared.
The introduction of the motor
coach is about to replace the
horse-drawn brake.

RAMSGATE

The Seafront c1880 R7302

We are looking from the eastern arm of the harbour. Ramsgate seafront was to see many developments over the coming years. On the extreme right, the railway station would become an amusement arcade, and in 1904, the Pavilion would be built nearby. The seafront buildings between the Obelisk and the Clock House would in time all be demolished; they were storehouses, the Trustees' Committee Rooms and the harbourmaster's house, all situated in the pier yard. Eventually, the ancient dredger would also be scrapped.

RAMSGATE
The Harbour 1892
ZZZ03387

The marquee was erected in the old stonemasons' yard by Christ Church and was used for mission services. To its right is the stone obelisk erected to celebrate George IV's proclamation that the harbour should be designated 'Royal' after the warm welcome he received from Ramsgate people on his arrival and departure in 1821. Local townsfolk refer to it as the 'Royal Toothpick'.

RAMSGATE, *The West Pier Lighthouse 1901* 48035c

Built in 1843 to the design of John Shaw, this lighthouse replaced an earlier one, built between 1792 and 1802. Constructed of 1,660 cubic feet of Portland stone, the 1843 lighthouse cost £1,000 to build. It has the Latin words 'perfugium miseris' cut into the stonework below its lantern; this apt quotation means 'shelter for the distressed'. In the background to the left of the lighthouse we can just see the Old Paragon swimming baths set into the cliff-face.

THE PAVILION AND THE SANDS

RAMSGATE
The Pavilion and the Harbour c1920 68461

The year 2004 was the 100th anniversary of the Royal
Victoria Pavilion, locally known as 'the Pav'. It was
designed by Mr S D Adshead, and cost £40,000 to build.
Originally a theatre with a sundeck, it was later used for
open-air dancing. Wintertime saw it become a cinema.
The lift to the right was opened in 1908.

▶ **RAMSGATE**
The Pavilion 1906 53467

Numerous shops were installed in the Pavilion complex. This view shows (to the left) a poster advertising Bailey's Central Pharmacy. More interesting are the three windows to the left of this poster; these belonged to Mr Short, a local photographer, whose photographs adorned these windows in neat rows.

◄ **RAMSGATE**
The Beach c1880 12731

The beach is overlooked by the Georgian houses of Wellington Crescent. In the centre is the Sands station, owned by the London, Chatham & Dover Railway, which opened on 5 October 1863. The low building extending from the left is the Colonnade, which was demolished by a storm in 1897 and replaced by the Royal Pavilion in 1904. In 1899, the South Eastern and the London, Chatham & Dover Railways combined to become the South Eastern & Chatham Railway, nicknamed 'the slow, easy and comfortable railway'.

▶ **RAMSGATE**
The Beach 1907 58272

The sands were a two-hour train ride from London. It was a children's summer playground. Bathing machines crowd the water's edge, and Barns's refreshment stall (background, centre left) vies with Mumfords the baker's nearby. Various carts dispense ice creams, sticky buns, and toffee apples, whilst the photographer busily produces your image on tin—his van is in the centre of the crowd. Ellinsons Entertainers, Punch and Judy and Harold Gold and his Yachtsmen entertained visitors. This crowded scene shows Ramsgate at its peak as a traditional English resort. In the background to the right is Ramsgate's iron pier, whilst to the extreme left is the Pavilion sundeck .

◀ **RAMSGATE**
Sands Station c1920
68460x

The Harbour, or Sands, station dominated Ramsgate beach from the time it was constructed. It covered the site that had once been the coastguard station, which was transferred to the East Cliff. The station was reached by a tunnel dug out of the chalk cliff measuring nearly a mile long. The tunnel ended on the outskirts of Ramsgate.

▲ **RAMSGATE,** *The Beach c1920* 68460c

It is low tide, and most of the bathing machines are high and dry, with the beach quite empty. In the background is the Promenade Pier, whose chequered life was short. Opened on 31 July 1881, it was 300 feet long and 30 feet wide. On 16 March 1884, it was sold by auction to its contractors for £2,000. After various fires and collisions, it was demolished in 1930.

◀ **RAMSGATE**
The Beach 1927 80370

In 1926, the Sands railway station closed and was converted to amusement arcades housing hundreds of slot machines; there was also a helter-skelter and a skating rink. The complex was known as Pleasureland. In the 1900s, many Sundays saw the Sands Mission holding religious services by the station. It is a strange fact that many old laws remain on the statute books; one still standing forbids bathing on Ramsgate beach.

THE TOWN

RAMSGATE, *Harbour Street c1920* ZZZ03388

Originally known as Waterside or East End, this was a busy thoroughfare. On the right was a grocer's, Pearks stores, with to its right Boots Cash Chemist. In the distance we can just see the tower of the parish church of St George. There are a variety of shops in Harbour Street, from Richardson's Hotel and Dixon & Baxter, the veterinary surgeons, to Timothy White's, who shared No 6 with McDonald Ltd, artificial teeth-makers.

▲ **RAMSGATE**
The Town Hall c1930 ZZZ03389

Situated at the cross-roads of Queen Street, King Street, Harbour Street and the High Street, the Town Hall was erected in 1839 at a cost of £1,239. Market stalls stood beneath the Council Chambers, and as far back as 1785, a market house existed on this site. The Town Hall was demolished in 1955 and replaced by new shops.

◄ **RAMSGATE**
Nos 120 & 122 King Street 1910 ZZZ03391

King Street used to be called North End, and was the first street in Ramsgate to have shops. The two shops depicted here are Daniel Hawkes, a fishmonger, and Mrs E J Bartlett, a wardrobe dealer, who shared her shop with Fred Emery, a confectioner.

RAMSGATE
The Market Place 1950
ZZZ03390

It is 'all hands to the pumps' as floodwater some six inches deep is desperately swept down the drains. To the right is King Street and the Red Lion, the oldest inn in the town, then a Truman's public house, followed by the Central Stores, and then H Wood & Co, the butcher's, Abbots Hill, and lastly Paynes, the greengrocer's.

RAMSGATE
*The Town Hall and
Queen Street 1907*
ZZZ03392

On 6 August 1907, French
dignitaries visited Ramsgate;
they can be seen passing the
old Town Hall into Queen
Street to a tumultuous
welcome from the townsfolk.
It is a sad fact that almost the
entire row of buildings to the
left has been demolished.

RAMSGATE, *No 32 Queen Street c1920* ZZZ03393

Situated half way between York Street and old Leopold Street, Murphy Francis's shoe shop was sole agent (pun intended!)
for Queen boots and shoes. This shop sold men's boots from 14s 9d to 15s 6d per pair, and also boasted a French boot and
shoe department.

RAMSGATE
High Street 1915 ZZZ03394

Once called the West End, from 1790 this street became the High Street. This view shows the Bull & George Hotel after it had received a direct hit from a bomb dropped by a Zeppelin on the night of 17 May 1915. This damage later caused the hotel to be demolished, and in 1920 the Woolworth's store was constructed on the vacant site.

71

RAMSGATE
High Street c1913 ZZZ03395

Here we see three of eight classical-style statues holding lanterns which stood at the junction of the High Street and George Street outside Sangers Amphitheatre and Hotel between 1911 and 1913. Six statues were removed and erected outside the Hall by the sea in Margate; the other two remained until 1939. There was controversy surrounding these figures: in 1908, Alderman Gwyn called them 'an eyesore and a disfigurement'. Lord George Sanger had seen the originals of the statues in Paris outside the Grand Opera House in 1883, and had eight replicas cast, paying £50 per figure for the transport and erection of these statues. Opposite is Lloyds Bank, which moved to new premises in 1928, renting the building to the NatWest Bank. The piano sign next door denotes Golden & Wind's premises.

RAMSGATE
The Fire-damaged Palace Theatre, High Street 1946 ZZZ03396

Thursday 21 June 1946 saw this scene at the Palace Theatre. Behind the safety curtain is nothing but desolation; the stage is littered with burnt debris, whilst scenery, including palm trees and a leaning lamp-post, seem to have survived. It is sad that the Palace was later to succumb to demolition in 1961. Man achieved what the fire could not, and the Palace was turned into a supermarket.

RAMSGATE, *J Dilnot, 60 High Street 1885* ZZZ03397

Situated on the opposite corner of George Street to the Palace was John Dilnot, a greengrocer and fruiterer's established in 1844. When this photograph was taken, this shop sold one pound of mushrooms for 3½d. Mr John Dilnot himself is thought to be the man standing in the doorway.

MADEIRA WALK
AND EAST CLIFF

RAMSGATE, *Madeira Walk 1901* 48042

Before 1895, Ramsgate's East Cliff was only accessible by walking up the narrow path to Albion Place or along the promenade to Augusta Steps. The Royal Albion Hotel had to be partially demolished to build a short, sharp incline known as Madeira Walk, which opened to the public on 6 April, 1895. Because space did not permit a gentler slope, the road had to be steep and winding. In 1901, the first trams ran linking the major towns of Thanet, and with them came numerous accidents on this precipitous road.

RAMSGATE
Madeira Walk, Waterfall 1905
48043

Madeira Walk was hewn out of chalk. The work began in 1892. This feature built by the road was an artificial waterfall and rustic bridge, with rocks giving the impression of a mountain scene. Later, with the widespread use of electricity, lights which changed to various colours were placed behind the running water. What is not generally known is that the rocks here are totally man-made from a special mix of sand, cement and an unknown ingredient—its trade name was Pulhamite. Madeira Walk cost nearly £60,000 to build, and because of the cost, the waterfall was dubbed 'the rate-payers' tears'.

RAMSGATE, *From Albion Place c1920* 68462

We are looking towards the West Cliff. On the left is the cupola of the old Customs House. The near-empty Harbour is the result of many fishing smacks lost during the First World War; the remainder transferred elsewhere. Just visible in the centre on the horizon is the tidal ball. When the ball is at the top of the mast it denotes that there is more than 10 feet of water between the pier heads of the outer harbour.

RAMSGATE, *The Grotto, Madeira Walk 1907* 58276

The Grotto, on the left as one descends the walk, has always been a place for children to play hide and seek. Behind in the distance are the houses of Albion Place. Albion House was for some time the holiday residence for Princess Victoria before she became Queen.

RAMSGATE
Augusta Road 1901
ZZZ03398

This road is named after Lady Augusta Murray, daughter of the 4th Earl and Countess of Dunmore. In 1817, then Lady d'Ameland, she purchased the Truro Estate. Her son and daughter were given the name d'Este, and in later years they sold large parts of the estate to Edward Welby Pugin. Various roads were named after the family - hence d'Este, Truro and Augusta Roads.

RAMSGATE, *Victoria Parade 1901* 48038

This broad parade, named after Queen Victoria, runs along the East Cliff in front of Wellington Crescent and the lawns. Erected in the middle of the green was an oak statue of Wellington, constructed by a shipwright, William Miller. It was later burnt down, some say by a drunken Irishman who objected to the Duke's politics. A well-known resident was Sir Charles Warren, an army commander in the Boer War, and Chief Superintendent of the Metropolitan Police during the hunt for Jack the Ripper.

RAMSGATE
The Granville Hotel 1901
48039

This was originally a terrace of very large houses built by Edward Welby Pugin. They failed to sell, and the terrace was converted to a hotel in 1869. In 1873, Pugin was bankrupted. Edmund Davis, who lived in Sowell Street, St Peter's, bought the building; he added a concert hall and baths and landscaped Victoria Gardens. It was used as a Canadian hospital in the First World War, and during the Second World War, in November 1940, it was bombed, and has never recovered its former 'sparkle'.

RAMSGATE, *Victoria Gardens Entrance c1920* 68463x

This is a typical 1920s British holiday scene. Both children clasp the toy of the era, a wooden hoop. Both gentlemen wear suits and bow ties, and everyone wears a hat. The four iron bollards replaced the earlier turnstile which charged a small entry fee to the gardens.

RAMSGATE
Victoria Gardens, the Kiosk c1920 68463c

Built around 1874, this building housed the attendant who took the monies at the
turnstile for entry into the gardens. When the gardens were purchased by the Borough
Council, the turnstile was removed, but the kiosk remained. Used as a newspaper kiosk,
it also sold sweets and postcards, and displayed a copy of the Borough Bye Laws.

79

▼ **RAMSGATE,** *The Hotel Saint Cloud 1901* 48040

Built between 1881 and 1882, these eight large houses were known as Granville Terrace.
In 1897, a Mr Robert Stacey bought the first five houses and converted them into the Hotel
Saint Cloud. Mr Stacey sold the hotel in 1919, and Mr J W Aptommas renamed it San Clu.
On Thursday 25 October 1928, a disastrous fire demolished three buildings, and what
remained became the San Clu Hotel. Today, it is the Comfort Inn.

▶ **RAMSGATE**
East Cliff Road 1916
ZZZ03399

As we look down the road
leading to Granville Marina,
we can see the sandbags and
barbed wire which were
placed here to prevent any
person approaching the
marina or the harbour during
the First World War. The
harbour became a naval
station known as HMS
Fervent. The central building
was known as The
Establishment, and part of the
building housed the Electric
Picture Palace.

◄ **RAMSGATE**
The View from East Cliff c1920 68464

To the right stand the Granville and San Clu Hotels (nearest to the camera). After acquiring the Granville, Edward Davies realised that the only access to the sands was by Augusta Steps. With the aid of the architect T J Winperis, in under a year he had built the Marina and Marina Road, which opened on 5 July 1877. Against the cliff-face to the right stands Ramsgate's first lift, which opened on 5 August 1908.

► **RAMSGATE**
The Beach and East Cliff c1920
68465

Beyond the marina and Marina Road was Golden Sands. Here in 1913/14 Ramsgate Corporation added steps to the sands and built Ramsgate Bathing Station. It was more popular with the locals, because it was away from the main beach. The prominent building on the cliff was part of Victoria Gardens.

RAMSGATE
East Cliff Bathing Station 1920 ZZZ03400

What a contrast a year can make now that the war is well and truly over. A beach photographer
(far left) advertises photographs at three for 2s or six for 3s 6d, and tea or coffee is for sale at 2d a cup.
Thomson & Wotton's brewery acquired this site and built an open-air swimming pool of championship
dimensions, which opened in July 1935. However, today it is a car park.

RAMSGATE
The Montefiore Mausoleum 1928 ZZZ03401

Built for Lady Judith, Sir Moses's wife, who died on 24 September 1862, the mausoleum is a copy of the legendary tomb of Rachel near Bethlehem. Sir Moses lived in East Cliff Lodge, and presented the mayor's chain to the town when it became a Corporation. He died in July 1885 at the age of 100 years and 10 months, and lies with his wife in the mausoleum, which is lit by an eternal flame.

DUMPTON GAP

RAMSGATE, *The Brown Jug Inn c1880* ZZZ03402

This dates back as far as the late 18th century, and was formerly known as the Queen's Arms Tap; it changed to the Brown Jug during the Napoleonic era. At the time of this photograph, it was owned by Mr J Saunders, and it was a watering-hole for the brakes which visited Dumpton Park, which was then situated behind the pub. A small brown jug stands over the entrance, and to the right the inn sign shows a brown jug.

RAMSGATE
Dumpton Gap 1894
34194

Dumpton lies within the urban boundaries of St Peter's and Broadstairs; its earlier name, 'Dodemayton', has long been forgotten, as has the hermit Pettit, who lived in a cave at Dumpton. He masqueraded as a religious man, but was found drunk in Ramsgate and duly disappeared. In 1914, a continental telephone cable to Ostend was installed, which came ashore at Dumpton.

RAMSGATE, *Westwood Cross 2004* ZZZ03403

With the union of the three towns of Ramsgate, Margate and Broadstairs under Thanet District Council, it is not surprising that a major shopping complex is being developed at Westwood, virtually in a central position to the community. Is this a pointer for the future of Ramsgate, and the rest of the Thanet towns?

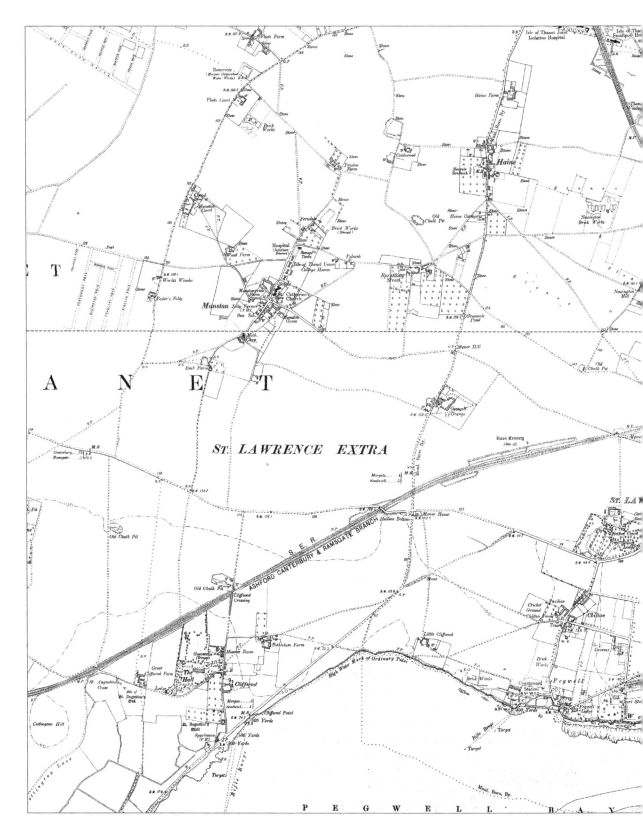

ORDNANCE SURVEY MAP *showing Ramsgate and surrounding areas c1900*

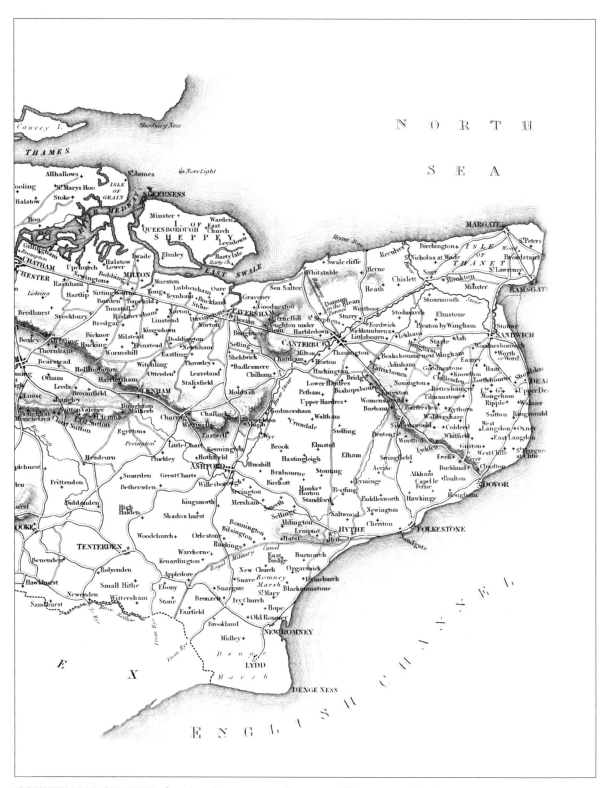

COUNTY MAP OF KENT *showing Ramsgate and surrounding areas c1850*

INDEX

NAMES OF PRE-PUBLICATION BUYERS

The following people have kindly supported this book by subscribing to copies before publication.

Mrs K A Affel (nee Williams), Philadelphia

The Allinson Family, Ramsgate

To Andrew, Happy Memories from Mum

Yvonne Anning, Ramsgate, for S & M Dorman Families

Anthony Atkins, Broadstairs

Lorraine June Attwell, Ramsgate

Graham Edward Attwell, Ramsgate

Ron Baker & Family, Ramsgate

In memory of Charles & Annie Banbury, Ramsgate

Lt Col M C & Mrs J I Barrett, Ramsgate

Mrs Maureen P Basilio

John & Jean Baynton, Ramsgate

BBC Radio Kent in Ramsgate on 104.2 fm

Mr & Mrs Belcher, Broadstairs

Mr J Bell, Ramsgate & Mrs A L Stubberfield, Ramsgate

Mrs Julie Blake, Moomins Town, Ramsgate

Mr A L Bootes, Ramsgate

70th Birthday, 9th Feb 2005, Ted Borley

To our Daughter Angela Bracey, with love

To our Son Vincent Bracey, with love

Happy 70th Bronie from Rene, Ron, Pat & Kate

To my husband, Harold T Brown, love Sue Brown, Ramsgate

Roy Brown, Ramsgate

In memory of J A D Browning

Peter Buckman, Broadstairs

Mrs Sheila Bywaters

David S Campany, Ramsgate

David P Carey, Ramsgate

Carol's Book of Ramsgate

Jan Chamberlain, Ramsgate

Roger Champion

Mrs Winifred Champs, Ramsgate

Mr & Mrs S G Clarke, Ramsgate

Linda & Bruce Collyer of Ramsgate

In memory of Hilda Coombs of Ramsgate

To Alf Cooper on your 75th Birthday

June & Chris Cork

To my sister Gwen Cote, USA, love Alan

Howard Cousins, Ramsgate

Ron & Pat Cox, Ramsgate

The Cunningham Family, Ramsgate

Mavis Darch

Jacqueline & Eric Davies, Broadstairs

Mr & Mrs R Davies, Ramsgate

Mr & Mrs R J Davies, West Yorkshire

Raymond, Marion & Neil Dawson, Ramsgate

Best Wishes to Mike Domaille

Mr & Mrs R Dorling

David & Doris Dorman, Ramsgate

Michael & Shirley Dorman, Broadstairs

L S Dyer, Kent Terrace, Ramsgate

Peter Edmunds

Loving thoughts for Andrew J Edwards from Bernard, Josephine, Bernice and Luke Edwards

To my son, Luke James Edwards, Deal, love Mum

Mr & Mrs R Edwards, North Wales

Eileen Eke, Ramsgate

Elliott & Bradley

John Embleton, an Unforgettable Dad xx

David Evans, Ramsgate

The Reverend Stanley & Mrs Marie Evans

In memory of Charles Farley, Ramsgate

David Anthony Fasham, Ramsgate

A Tribute to the Fishing Smacks & Crews

The Ford Family, Ramsgate

The Fullagar Family of Ramsgate, CT11 OBP

The Fullbrook Family, Ramsgate

Ian Fuller & Family from 16.01.2004

Albert W G Fuller, Ramsgate

The Gambrill Family, Ramsgate

The Gander Family, Ramsgate

Leslie & Dorothy Gaymer, Ramsgate 1945

Douglas J Gifford

Alfie & Sheila Goldfinch, Ramsgate

Ken J Gray, Ramsgate

Colin Greenstreet

Esmond Greenstreet

George Greenstreet

Mr Philip Greenstreet, Ramsgate

Brian & Gillian Harris

Stephen Henry Harris

Kenneth P Hawkes, Ramsgate

Marion E Hawkes, Ramsgate

J E, M E, D M, S R & R I Hedges, Ramsgate

Anthony & Maureen Hill, Ramsgate

Leonard & Frances Hill, Ramsgate

To Daphne & Patrick Hope from Mum 2005

Mr & Mrs T J Horne, Ramsgate

The Hougham Family, Ramsgate

Happy 50th Birthday Howard from Tina & Daz

D C Hoyle & Family

Mr J A Huckel & Mrs A K Huckle, Ramsgate

R W Hudson, Ramsgate

Michael John Hudson, Ramsgate

Marc Ingram, Artillery Rd, Ramsgate

Frederick W G James

The Johnson Family, Ramsgate

Sally & Pete Johnson of Ramsgate

W J & S E Johnson

To Keith, Happy Birthday, love always, Lynn

The Keys Family, Ramsgate

Leslie & June Kirkden, Ramsgate

Dennis Lawrence Knight, Ramsgate

In memory of George & Irene Knowler, Sandwich

Jeanne & Maurice Kreisberg & Family

Andrew Grant Kurtis and Family

John Lacy & Shirley Lacy

The Lambeth Family, Ramsgate

John Percy Larkins, Ramsgate

Mr Kevin Laurence

To Julie Lemare, love from Mum and Dad

For my Mum, Mary Lincoln, Ramsgate, from Kathy

Tony Lincoln, born Ramsgate 1950

Patricia & Arthur Lucas of Ramsgate

In memory of a true friend, Mr B McEvely

Mr & Mrs Lyne, Ramsgate

The McManus Family, Ramsgate

Memories of Steve Maiden 1983-2004

In memory of Rhoda Major, from Pat & Kate

In memory of Doris Martin, born 1925, died 2000

To Bill, in memory of Marie & Frank Cyril Maxted

William David Maxted, beloved of Ethel & Pam

The May Family

Joseph R May, Ramsgate

John Mills, from a loving family

Ken Milner & Family, Ramsgate

Brenda Mobbs

Joyce & Dennis Moodey, Ramsgate

Jill Moorby, Ramsgate with love Gabby

Davis & Margaret Morgan

Mr & Mrs A T Morley

Mr Stephen Morrell of Ramsgate

Peter Morrison, Ramsgate

Andrew David Newing, Ramsgate

Newlands Primary School 2005

The Newman Family

In Memory of Rose & Eric Newton

Mr & Mrs D P & D P O'Neill of Ramsgate

Peter O'Sullivan, Ramsgate

Harold & Inez Palmer

John & Sandra Parker, Ramsgate

To Ian J Pearson on his Birthday

Darron Pettman, Ramsgate

Frank Phillips

To Mr D Picton, Ramsgate, on his Birthday

John & Joan Pidduck, Ramsgate

Mrs Rose Pidduck, Ramsgate

Steve & Christine Pidduck, Ramsgate

Miss J A Porter, Ramsgate

David John Preston, Ramsgate

Mum, Mrs H Reeves & Family, Ramsgate

In memory of Herby & Dave Reeves, Ramsgate

Mrs Janet Reid, Ramsgate

Mr J J H Reynolds of Ramsgate

David T Richards, Ramsgate

The Richardson Family - Ramsgate 2005

Mel & John Roden, Ramsgate

David Charles Rogers, Margate

Betty & Len Rutt, Ramsgate

Pamela J Salcombe, Ramsgate

To Sarah, Happy Memories from Mum

David James Savage, Ramsgate, Kent

Mr D T & Mrs C G Sayer, Ramsgate

William T Sayer

Steven J Scholes, Ramsgate

The Selby Family, Ramsgate

Gwendoline Shane (nee Board)

In memory of Van George Sharman, Ramsgate

In memory of Joyce & Will Sharp

Frank Shaw, Ramsgate

Mr C & Mrs M E Simpson of Ramsgate

The Simpson Family, Ramsgate

Daphne & Peter Smith, Ramsgate

A Standley

K Standley

To Stephen, Happy Memories from Mum

In memory of Elvy & Elizabeth Esther Stickels, Ramsgate

The Stiff Family, Ramsgate

Martyn E Stokes, Ramsgate

Alan, Tina & Aaron Stone, Ramsgate

For my Son, Joseph James Strevens

Mr B A & Mrs D J Stubbings, Ramsgate

Joyce H Sudds, Ramsgate

Joan & Phil Swartz, America

P Taylor & M J Taylor, Ramsgate

In memory of Thomas Taylor, Ramsgate

Andrew Thomas, La Belle, Alliance Square

The Thomas Collins Family, Ramsgate

Mr Roy Thomas, Prospect Terrace

Wyndham, Jane, Jan & David Thomas, Ramsgate

Andrew & Rita Tobin from Ramsgate

In memory of our Dad, S Todd, 1918, Ramsgate

Paul Tuddenham, Ramsgate

Warren Tuddenham, Ramsgate

Ian J Turner, Ramsgate

Alexandra Tyler

To Marjorie from John & Vivien Walford

To Neil Waller on his 40th Birthday, Mum

Steve Ward, Mayor of Ramsgate 2004/2005

Mrs C A Webb of Hayes, Bromley

Mr & Mrs J Wenbourne, Ramsgate

Mr & Mrs M E Wheatley-Ward, Ramsgate

Terry Wheeler, Ramsgate, Kent

Mrs J Williams (nee Fuller-Barrs), Ramsgate

Joanne Williams, Ramsgate

To Mick Williams of Ramsgate, 'Happy Birthday'

Primrose M Williamson, Ramsgate

Barbara Wood (nee Tilbrook)

Albert J Wyles

Bob & Jan Xarim, Toll Gate Kiosk, Ramsgate

FREE PRINT OF YOUR CHOICE

Mounted Print
Overall size 14 x 11 inches (355 x 280mm)

Choose any Frith photograph in this book.
Simply complete the Voucher opposite and return it with your remittance for £2.25 (to cover postage and handling) and we will print the photograph of your choice in SEPIA (size 11 x 8 inches) and supply it in a cream mount with a burgundy rule line (overall size 14 x 11 inches).
Please note: photographs with a reference number starting with a "Z" are not Frith photographs and cannot be supplied under this offer.
Offer valid for delivery to one UK address only.

PLUS: **Order additional Mounted Prints at HALF PRICE - £7.49 each** (normally £14.99)
If you would like to order more Frith prints from this book, possibly as gifts for friends and family, you can buy them at half price (with no additional postage and handling costs).

PLUS: **Have your Mounted Prints framed**
For an extra £14.95 per print you can have your mounted print(s) framed in an elegant polished wood and gilt moulding, overall size 16 x 13 inches (no additional postage and handling required).

IMPORTANT!

These special prices are only available if you use this form to order . You must use the ORIGINAL VOUCHER on this page (no copies permitted). We can only despatch to one UK address. This offer cannot be combined with any other offer.

Send completed Voucher form to:
The Francis Frith Collection, Frith's Barn, Teffont, Salisbury, Wiltshire SP3 5QP

CHOOSE A PHOTOGRAPH FROM THIS BOOK

 *Voucher* *for FREE and Reduced Price Frith Prints*

Please do not photocopy this voucher. Only the original is valid, so please fill it in, cut it out and return it to us with your order.

Picture ref no	Page no	Qty	Mounted @ £7.49	Framed + £14.95	Total Cost £
		1	Free of charge*	£	£
			£7.49	£	£
			£7.49	£	£
			£7.49	£	£
			£7.49	£	£
			£7.49	£	£

Please allow 28 days for delivery.
Offer available to one UK address only

* Post & handling	£2.25
Total Order Cost	£

Title of this book . . . .
I enclose a cheque/postal order for £ . . . .
made payable to 'The Francis Frith Collection'

OR please debit my Mastercard / Visa / Maestro / Amex card, details below

Card Number

Issue No (Maestro only)   Valid from (Maestro)

Expires   Signature

Name Mr/Mrs/Ms . . . .
Address . . . .
. . . .
. . . .
. . . . Postcode . . . .
Daytime Tel No . . . .
Email . . . .

ISBN: 1-85937-627-X   Valid to 31/12/07

Free Print – see overleaf

Would you like to find out more about Francis Frith?

We have recently recruited some entertaining speakers who are happy to visit local groups, clubs and societies to give an illustrated talk documenting Frith's travels and photographs. If you are a member of such a group and are interested in hosting a presentation, we would love to hear from you.

Our speakers bring with them a small selection of our local town and county books, together with sample prints. They are happy to take orders. A small proportion of the order value is donated to the group who have hosted the presentation. The talks are therefore an excellent way of fundraising for small groups and societies.

Can you help us with information about any of the Frith photographs in this book?

We are gradually compiling an historical record for each of the photographs in the Frith archive. It is always fascinating to find out the names of the people shown in the pictures, as well as insights into the shops, buildings and other features depicted.

If you recognize anyone in the photographs in this book, or if you have information not already included in the author's caption, do let us know. We would love to hear from you, and will try to publish it in future books or articles.

Our production team

Frith books are produced by a small dedicated team at offices in the converted Grade II listed 18th-century barn at Teffont near Salisbury, illustrated above. Most have worked with the Frith Collection for many years. All have in common one quality: they have a passion for the Frith Collection. The team is constantly expanding, but currently includes:

Paul Baron, Phillip Brennan, Jason Buck, John Buck, Ruth Butler, Heather Crisp, David Davies, Louis du Mont, Isobel Hall, Lucy Hart, Julian Hight, Peter Horne, James Kinnear, Karen Kinnear, Tina Leary, Stuart Login, David Marsh, Lesley-Ann Millard, Sue Molloy, Glenda Morgan, Wayne Morgan, Sarah Roberts, Kate Rotondetto, Dean Scource, Eliza Sackett, Terence Sackett, Sandra Sampson, Adrian Sanders, Sandra Sanger, Julia Skinner, Miles Smith, Lewis Taylor, Shelley Tolcher, Lorraine Tuck, David Turner, Amanita Wainwright and Ricky Williams.